Logged Out: My Digital Detox Memoir and the Journey Back to Real Life

A Personal Journey of Breaking Free from Digital Addiction, Rebuilding Human Connection, and Finding Meaning Beyond Screens with digital minimalism

Elliot Hayes

Contents

Foreword   v

Part 1
The Digital Cage

1. Hooked on the Scroll   3
2. The Erosion of Presence   7
3. The Breaking Point   12

Part 2
The Great Unplugging

4. The Digital Detox Begins   19
5. Confronting the Void   25
6. Relearning Human Connection   31

Part 3
The Awakening

7. Rediscovering the Real World   41
8. The Challenges of Staying Unplugged   48

Part 4
A New Way of Living

9. The Unexpected Lessons   55
10. Rewired for Good   63

Your Invitation to Unplug   69

Author's Note   71

Foreword

We live in an age of **constant connection**—but somehow, we've never felt more disconnected.

Our attention is fragmented, our relationships are strained, and our ability to simply *be* has been replaced by an insatiable need to consume, share, and engage.

For years, I was trapped in this cycle. I woke up to notifications, fell asleep to the blue glow of my screen, and measured my worth in likes, comments, and online interactions. And yet, beneath all of it, I felt *empty*.

That's why I decided to walk away.

This book isn't just about quitting social media or taking a break from technology. It's about something deeper— **reclaiming your time, your attention, and your sense of self.**

It's about remembering what life feels like when you're fully present for it.

Foreword

This is my journey of unplugging. Of breaking free. Of rediscovering what truly matters.

And if you've ever felt trapped by the digital world—if you've ever felt like your life is slipping away in a blur of screens and notifications—then this book is for you.

It's an invitation to disconnect. To slow down. To experience life beyond the algorithm.

And most of all, it's a reminder that **you are not your screen.**

You are real.

Your life is real.

And the best moments are waiting for you—on the other side of the scroll.

Part 1
The Digital Cage

Chapter 1
Hooked on the Scroll

I don't remember exactly when the internet became my second home. Maybe it was the first time I heard the dial-up tone screeching through our old desktop computer, signaling a connection to something bigger than my small, familiar world. Or maybe it was the day I made my first social media account, crafting an online version of myself that, in time, felt more real than the person staring back at me in the mirror.

What I do remember is the feeling. The thrill of logging in. The rush of seeing a new message notification. The instant gratification of a "like." These little bursts of dopamine became the rhythm of my life, a silent but persistent beat that dictated my moods, my choices, and even my sense of self.

The Birth of an Addiction

It started innocently enough. Like most people my age, I grew up with technology evolving around me, seamlessly weaving itself into my daily routine. At first, the internet was a tool—

something to help with homework, a way to stay in touch with friends after school, a place to explore interests. But slowly, without me realizing it, the balance shifted. The internet stopped being a resource and became a refuge.

By my teenage years, social media had taken center stage. I remember the excitement of setting up my first profile—choosing a profile picture, crafting a bio that made me sound effortlessly cool, adding friends like collecting trading cards. It wasn't just about being online; it was about being *seen*.

What started as casual curiosity morphed into something else entirely. I began measuring my worth by the engagement my posts received. A photo that got 100 likes meant I was funny, attractive, or interesting. A post that got ignored? That was a gut punch, a quiet whisper of "you're not good enough."

How Technology Shaped My Life

Morning routines used to involve stretching, making breakfast, and maybe some quiet reflection before starting the day. But soon, my mornings became a frantic dive into my phone—checking notifications before my feet even touched the floor, scrolling through updates while brushing my teeth, responding to messages before I had spoken a word to another human in real life.

Social interactions changed too. Hanging out with friends no longer meant full, undivided attention. Our conversations were punctuated by screen glances, interrupted by beeps and buzzes, and sometimes silenced altogether as we sat side by side, scrolling separately in a shared space. I told myself I was "connected" to hundreds of people, yet I often felt lonelier than ever.

At night, I'd lie in bed, endlessly swiping, scrolling through feeds of people living seemingly perfect lives—vacations, parties, career successes, relationships. It didn't matter that I knew social media was a highlight reel, that behind every smiling photo was a reality I wasn't seeing. The comparison trap was inescapable. I always felt like I was falling behind.

The Dopamine Trap

Every notification was a tiny hit of validation. A new message? Someone was thinking about me. A comment? I mattered. A flood of likes? I was accepted, popular, seen.

The platforms knew this, of course. They were designed this way. Every color, every feature, every algorithm—crafted to keep me engaged, to keep me craving the next small rush of pleasure. And I fell for it. Over and over again.

I noticed patterns. If I posted something and didn't get engagement fast enough, I'd delete it, as if the post itself was a failure and, by extension, so was I. If I saw someone else's life looking more exciting than mine, I'd feel the urge to post something too—anything—to prove I was just as happy, just as successful, just as *worthy*.

It wasn't about sharing moments anymore. It was about performance. It was about crafting an identity that was just polished enough to be admired but not so perfect that it felt fake. It was about maintaining the illusion of a life well-lived, even if it meant spending more time documenting life than actually living it.

The Unseen Cost

I told myself it wasn't a problem. Everyone was online. This was just how the world worked now. But deep down, I knew something was off.

I noticed how much harder it became to focus. Reading a book? Impossible. My brain craved the fast-paced stimulation of endless scrolling.

I noticed how my self-esteem rose and fell based on the reactions I received online. A compliment in real life was nice, but digital praise? That was intoxicating.

I noticed how real-world conversations became more difficult. Face-to-face interactions required patience, active listening, and real engagement. But I had trained my brain to operate in bursts—140-character thoughts, ten-second videos, quick reactions. Slow, meaningful conversations felt almost unnatural.

Worst of all, I noticed how much time I had lost. Hours, days, years—spent staring at a screen, living through the lives of others while my own life quietly slipped away.

I didn't know it yet, but I was trapped. And getting out wouldn't be easy.

Chapter 2
The Erosion of Presence

I used to think I was good at multitasking. I could hold a conversation while checking my phone, scroll through social media while watching a movie, respond to messages while sitting at dinner with friends. I told myself I was being efficient, staying connected, keeping up with everything all at once. But the truth was, I wasn't really present in any of it.

I was everywhere and nowhere at the same time.

The Gradual Disappearance of Attention

It didn't happen overnight. I didn't wake up one day and suddenly find myself incapable of focus. It was slow, subtle, unnoticeable at first—until one day, I realized I couldn't remember the last time I had sat in silence without reaching for a screen.

I started noticing it in the small moments:

- **Conversations that felt disjointed.** Someone would be telling me a story, and I'd nod along, but my eyes would flicker down to my phone. My replies became automatic—"Yeah," "Totally," "That's crazy"—but I wasn't really hearing them.

- **Books that went unfinished.** I used to love reading, but suddenly, sitting down with a novel felt exhausting. My mind craved something faster, something easier to consume. A five-minute video. A quick-hit article. A TikTok that wrapped up a complex idea in 30 seconds.

- **Constant background noise.** Silence made me uncomfortable. I always needed something playing—a podcast, music, a YouTube video. Something to fill the space so I wouldn't have to sit alone with my thoughts.

It was as if my brain had been rewired for short bursts of stimulation, incapable of handling anything that required patience or sustained focus.

The Cost of Constant Distraction

I didn't just lose attention—I lost connection.

With friends. I started noticing how often we'd sit together, phones in hand, barely speaking. Even when we did talk, there was an unspoken agreement that checking notifications mid-conversation was acceptable. If a lull in the conversation lasted more than a few seconds, someone would pull out their phone, and the rest of us would follow. It was a chain reaction of disengagement.

With family. I'd visit home and sit at the dinner table, one hand scrolling under the table like an addict sneaking a hit.

My parents would ask about my life, and I'd give half-hearted responses while my mind drifted back to whatever was happening online.

With myself. I could no longer sit still without reaching for a screen. Waiting in line? Scroll. Walking down the street? Scroll. Using the bathroom? Scroll. Any moment of stillness felt like wasted time—time that could be filled with consuming something, even if it was just an endless loop of meaningless content.

I had mistaken connection for consumption. I wasn't engaging with the world; I was numbing myself to it.

The Illusion of Being Connected

Social media made me feel like I was close to people. I could see their lives unfold in real-time—vacations, milestones, everyday moments captured in snapshots. But it was a mirage.

I knew what my friends were doing, but I wasn't actually experiencing it with them. I knew what they were thinking, but only in the curated way they presented themselves online. When we finally met in person, there was less to say. "I saw your post," we'd say, as if that was a substitute for a real conversation.

And yet, I kept doing it. Checking in. Watching stories. Liking posts. Because if I didn't, I felt like I was missing something. Like I was fading into the background.

I convinced myself that this was just how the world worked now. That my relationships weren't suffering; they were just evolving. That being available 24/7 through a screen was the same as being *present*.

But deep down, I knew it wasn't.

When Presence Becomes a Performance

The real turning point came when I noticed how much of my life I was staging.

I wasn't just taking photos to capture memories—I was curating them for an audience. I'd be at a concert, but instead of enjoying the music, I'd be recording snippets for Instagram. I'd go on a trip, but instead of being in the moment, I'd be thinking about the perfect caption.

There was always a layer of performance, a constant awareness of how my life appeared through a screen. It wasn't enough to experience something—I had to document it, to validate it with digital proof that I was living.

And in doing so, I was missing the very life I was trying to capture.

The Breaking Point

One day, I was out with friends, sitting at an outdoor café. The conversation was light, but I wasn't really in it. My phone was on the table, face-up, and I kept glancing at it. No notifications. No messages. Just an itch to check, to refresh, to see if something new had happened in the digital world.

Then I looked up.

Everyone at the table was doing the same thing. Heads tilted down, fingers scrolling, eyes flicking between screens and reality.

No one was *here*.

And in that moment, something inside me shifted.

I had spent so much time trying to stay connected that I had completely disconnected from the only world that was real.

I didn't know it yet, but this was the beginning of my decision to unplug.

Chapter 3
The Breaking Point

I didn't quit cold turkey. No one does. Digital addiction isn't like a light switch you can just flip off. It's more like an invisible leash—sometimes slack, sometimes pulling you back with full force.

At first, I didn't even admit I had a problem. I told myself what everyone tells themselves: *This is just how the world works now. Everyone's on their phone. Everyone's online. It's normal.*

But deep down, I knew. I could feel the weight of it—this constant, nagging presence in my mind. The feeling of never being *fully* here. The growing anxiety when I wasn't connected. The sense that life was slipping away in a blur of notifications, scrolling, and digital noise.

Something had to change.

The Wake-Up Call

The moment that shook me wasn't dramatic. No life-or-death crisis, no intervention. Just a quiet realization that hit me harder than anything else.

I was sitting in my apartment, phone in hand, endlessly scrolling. My to-do list sat untouched beside me—emails to respond to, a book half-read, laundry waiting to be folded. It wasn't that I didn't have things to do; it was that my brain refused to engage with anything that required patience.

I glanced at the clock. **Three hours** had passed.

Three hours. Gone.

And for what?

I couldn't even remember what I had consumed in that time. Just a blur of memes, headlines, strangers' opinions, short videos I'd never think about again. I had disappeared into a digital fog, and when I resurfaced, I felt nothing but emptiness.

That was the first moment I genuinely asked myself: *Is this how I want to live?*

Failed Attempts at Control

Like any addiction, my first instinct was to negotiate with it. I didn't want to quit entirely; I just wanted to be *better* at managing it.

- **"I'll only check social media in the morning and at night."** (That lasted a day.)

- **"I'll turn off notifications."** (I still checked my phone compulsively.)

- **"I'll take a weekend off."** (And then made up for lost time on Monday.)

Every time I tried to cut back, I felt the pull of it even stronger. The itch to check, the fear of missing something, the strange sense of *who even am I if I'm not online?*

It wasn't just about technology—it was about identity. I had spent years shaping my digital self, curating the version of me that existed on the internet. And if I stepped away, what would be left?

The Breaking Point

The real breaking point came on a trip.

I had convinced myself that traveling would be different. That I'd be *present*, soaking in the experience, fully engaged with the world around me. But from the moment I arrived, I fell into the same pattern:

- Taking pictures not for myself, but for Instagram.

- Checking my phone between every major sight, every meal, every moment of stillness.

- Feeling a subtle, creeping anxiety if I was offline too long.

One evening, I found myself standing in front of one of the most beautiful sights I had ever seen—a sunset spilling gold and pink hues across the sky, the kind of moment that makes time slow down.

And what did I do?

I pulled out my phone.

Not just to take a photo, but to post it. To share it. To see the reaction.

As I stood there, staring at my screen while real life unfolded before me, a wave of shame hit me.

I wasn't *here*. I wasn't in this moment.

I was chasing a digital ghost of reality, sacrificing the present for the sake of validation.

I turned off my phone and put it in my bag.

And for the first time in years, I stood in silence. Just me, the sky, the world.

No screen. No distractions. No performance.

Just presence.

The Decision to Disconnect

That moment wasn't the end of my addiction, but it was the beginning of the end.

I realized something I had been avoiding for years: *I was losing my life to a screen.*

Not just time—*life*.

Real conversations. Real experiences. Real emotions. All of it dulled, blurred, half-lived because I was always half-somewhere else.

I knew I had to change. Not just for a day, not just as a temporary detox, but permanently.

I didn't want to be a prisoner to technology anymore. I wanted to reclaim my mind, my time, my sense of self.

And so, I made the decision: **I was going to unplug.**

Not forever. Not in some extreme, off-grid way.

But enough to break free. Enough to start living again.

Part 2
The Great Unplugging

Chapter 4
The Digital Detox Begins

Quitting the internet sounds easy in theory. Just turn off your phone, log out, and live your life. But when you've spent years hardwired to digital stimulation, breaking free feels like ripping out an organ. The instinct to check, to scroll, to fill every idle moment with something—*anything*—is so deeply ingrained that it doesn't disappear overnight.

Still, I knew I had to start somewhere.

Step One: Deleting the Triggers

The first thing I did was delete social media apps from my phone. Just holding down the icons and watching them disappear felt strange, like I was erasing part of my existence. My thumb hovered for a second before pressing "delete," my mind whispering excuses: *What if I need them for something? What if people think I'm ignoring them? What if I miss something important?*

But I deleted them anyway.

Then I went a step further.

I turned off notifications. I unfollowed accounts that made me feel inadequate. I removed shortcuts to social media from my browser. I set up screen limits. I even considered switching to a dumb phone.

And yet, despite all these changes, I caught myself *still* reaching for my phone out of habit. My brain didn't care that I had deleted the apps. It had been conditioned to seek stimulation, to fill silence, to escape boredom.

I wasn't just fighting technology. I was fighting my own mind.

The First Days: Withdrawal Hits

I didn't expect quitting social media to feel like withdrawal. But that's exactly what it was.

- I felt restless, like I had lost a limb. My hands kept reaching for my phone, only to realize there was nothing to check.

- I felt anxious, haunted by the idea that I was "falling behind." What if people were talking about me? What if I missed an important message?

- I felt *bored*. The kind of boredom I hadn't experienced in years—the deep, uncomfortable boredom that makes time stretch and forces you to sit with yourself.

For the first time in ages, there was no endless feed to distract me. Just silence. Just space.

And it was terrifying.

Learning to Sit with Stillness

I didn't know what to do with myself.

Without a screen to escape into, I had to actually *experience* my day in full. No skipping over dull moments with a quick scroll. No numbing out uncomfortable thoughts.

Mornings felt longer. Meals felt slower. Time itself seemed to stretch.

At first, it was unbearable. But then, something surprising happened: **I started noticing life again.**

I noticed the way sunlight streamed through my window in the morning. The way food actually *tasted* when I wasn't eating with one hand on my phone. The way my mind wandered into creativity when I let myself be bored.

I had spent years shoving every moment full of digital noise, never letting myself *just be*. And now, in the stillness, I was rediscovering something I didn't know I had lost.

Replacing the Scroll with Something Real

The hardest part of quitting technology wasn't the absence of social media—it was figuring out *what to do instead*.

Because the truth was, the internet had been filling my time. Without it, I had to confront the empty spaces in my day and find ways to fill them with something meaningful.

So, I started experimenting:

- **Reading books again.** At first, my mind struggled to focus. I craved the fast, bite-sized content I was used to. But over time, I re-learned how to lose myself in a story.

- **Journaling.** Instead of broadcasting my thoughts online, I wrote them down for myself. No likes, no comments, just raw, unfiltered reflection.

- **Going for walks without my phone.** Just me, the world, and my thoughts. No music, no podcasts—just the sound of my own footsteps.

- **Reconnecting with old hobbies.** Drawing, playing music, even just sitting outside and watching the world pass by.

At first, these things felt slow, even pointless. My brain still craved digital dopamine, the instant rush of notifications and updates.

But the longer I stayed away, the more I realized: *real life isn't supposed to be fast-paced and hyper-stimulating all the time.*

The beauty of life is in the quiet moments. And I had been missing them.

The Struggle of Real-World Connection

One of the hardest parts of my digital detox wasn't just changing my own habits—it was realizing how deeply technology had embedded itself into my relationships.

When I met up with friends, I noticed how often their eyes flickered down to their screens, mid-conversation. How many moments were interrupted by notifications. How hard it was to sit together without someone reaching for their phone.

For the first time, I was *aware* of it.

And I didn't know how to fix it.

I tried bringing it up, gently suggesting we put our phones away when we hung out. Some people agreed. Others laughed it off. "It's just how things are," they'd say. And I understood, because I used to think the same thing.

But now, I saw it differently. I saw how much we were losing—real conversations, real presence, real connection. And I wondered: *Was this just the way the world was now? Or was there still a way back?*

The First Glimpse of Freedom

After a few weeks without social media, something unexpected happened.

The restlessness faded. The anxiety quieted. The itch to check my phone wasn't as strong.

And in its place, I felt something I hadn't felt in a long time.

Peace.

I wasn't constantly comparing myself to others. I wasn't drowning in information. I wasn't being pulled in a hundred different directions by algorithms designed to keep me hooked.

I was just *here*. Living. Breathing. Experiencing the world in real-time.

For the first time in years, I felt like my mind belonged to me again.

And I knew: **I could never go back.**

Chapter 5
Confronting the Void

The first few days of my digital detox were like stepping into a different world—one that moved slower, one where silence wasn't immediately filled with distractions. It was refreshing, even exhilarating at times.

But then, the emptiness set in.

For the first time in years, I wasn't bombarded with notifications, endless scrolling, or the constant chatter of the online world. And without that noise, something unexpected happened: **I had to sit with myself.**

And I realized I had no idea how to do that.

The Uncomfortable Reality of Stillness

For years, I had used the internet to avoid something I hadn't even realized I was running from—**my own mind.**

Whenever I felt bored, anxious, or lonely, I reached for my phone. Every spare second of my life had been filled with something—tweets, videos, news updates, memes, messages. There was always a way to keep my brain occupied, to drown out whatever thoughts might creep in if I sat still for too long.

But now, there was nothing standing between me and those thoughts.

And at first, that terrified me.

I started noticing emotions I hadn't let myself feel. Unresolved anxieties, self-doubt, fears about the future—all the things I had shoved to the back of my mind came rushing forward.

The silence wasn't peaceful anymore. It was loud.

For the first time, I had to ask myself: *Without the internet to tell me what to think, what do I actually believe? Without social media to shape my identity, who am I really?*

I didn't have immediate answers. But I knew I had to start looking for them.

The Fear of Missing Out (FOMO) Hits Hard

One of the biggest struggles was **feeling disconnected.**

Even though I had made the decision to unplug, the world hadn't stopped moving. Friends were still posting. News was still breaking. Conversations were still happening online, and I wasn't part of them anymore.

And that messed with my head.

I'd sit in a coffee shop, watching people around me absorbed in their screens, and wonder what I was missing. What was happening in the world that I wasn't seeing? What messages were going unread?

I felt like I was disappearing. Like I had made myself invisible.

For a while, that feeling was unbearable.

But then, something shifted.

I asked myself: *What exactly am I afraid of missing?*

- Another person's vacation photos?
- Another round of arguments in the comments section?
- Another trending topic that would be forgotten in a week?

The truth was, I wasn't missing *life*—I was missing *noise*.

And the more I sat with that realization, the more I saw FOMO for what it really was: an illusion.

Real life was happening right in front of me. And I was finally starting to see it.

The Addiction to External Validation

One of the hardest things about quitting social media wasn't just breaking the habit of checking my phone.

It was breaking the habit of seeking validation.

For years, I had unconsciously trained myself to *need* digital approval. Likes, comments, messages—each one was a little hit of dopamine, a reassurance that I mattered, that people saw me, that I was relevant.

Without that constant feedback, I started feeling... invisible.

I posted something, and there was no reaction.

I had thoughts, and they stayed in my head instead of being broadcasted.

I did things, and no one online knew about them.

And that felt *strange*. Almost as if my experiences weren't real unless they were acknowledged by others.

That realization hit me hard.

Had I really reached a point where I needed strangers on the internet to validate my existence?

I had to relearn how to live without an audience.

To read a book and not share my thoughts on it.

To enjoy a sunset without posting a photo.

To do something meaningful without proving it to anyone else.

And slowly, I started reclaiming my sense of self—not as someone who performed for the internet, but as someone who simply *existed*.

Rediscovering the Joy of Doing Things for Myself

At some point, something shifted.

The silence that had once been deafening became peaceful.

The FOMO that had once gnawed at me became irrelevant.

The need for validation that had once controlled me started to fade.

And in its place, I found something unexpected: **joy.**

I started doing things just because I wanted to—not because they'd look good on social media, not because they'd get engagement, but simply because they made me happy.

- **I wrote for myself,** without worrying about how it would be received.
- **I walked without my phone,** letting my mind wander instead of filling it with distractions.
- **I sat with my thoughts,** no longer afraid of what they might tell me.

I realized that life felt *fuller* without the constant pressure to document and share every moment.

For the first time in years, I was experiencing life *as it was happening*—not through a screen, not for an audience, but for me.

The Turning Point

There was a day, maybe a month into my detox, when I went to a park with a book.

I sat on a bench, feeling the sun on my skin, watching people walk by, hearing the distant sounds of conversations and laughter.

And for the first time in as long as I could remember, I felt completely **at peace**.

No notifications.

No pressure to check in.

No fear of missing out.

Just me, fully present in the moment.

And I realized: *This is what I was missing all along.*

Not the latest updates.

Not the endless opinions of strangers.

Not the constant validation.

But **this.**

Real life.

Real presence.

Real connection with the world around me.

And for the first time, I knew that I had no desire to go back.

I had spent years trapped in the digital addiction trap, searching for meaning in pixels and posts.

But now, I was finally free.

And I wasn't looking back.

Chapter 6
Relearning Human Connection

When I first quit social media, I thought the hardest part would be the boredom—the absence of constant entertainment, the stillness where scrolling used to be.

I was wrong.

The hardest part was facing how much **technology had rewired the way I connected with people.**

Without the buffer of screens, conversations felt different. Hanging out with friends felt different. Even being alone with my thoughts felt different.

It wasn't just about unplugging from the internet.

It was about **learning how to be human again.**

The Digital Wall Between Us

Before my detox, I had convinced myself that I was **connected** to people. After all, I knew what was happening in their lives—who got a promotion, who was traveling, who was having a bad day. I sent emojis, reacted to their posts, left comments.

But I started to realize that **knowing about someone's life isn't the same as being a part of it.**

I knew my friends' updates, but I didn't know their struggles.

I knew their highlight reels, but I didn't know their quiet moments.

I knew their opinions on trending topics, but I didn't know how they were *really* doing.

Social media had given me the illusion of closeness, but in reality, I had been watching people's lives unfold from a distance—like a spectator instead of a participant.

I didn't just need to disconnect from the internet.

I needed to **reconnect with people.**

The Awkwardness of Real Conversations

The first time I hung out with a friend after deleting social media, I noticed something that made me uncomfortable:

Face-to-face conversation required more effort.

Without the ability to pause, edit, or multitask, I had to fully engage. I couldn't fill silences by glancing at my phone. I couldn't rely on a constant stream of memes and links to keep the conversation going.

And at first, I struggled.

I had gotten used to **digital communication**, where conversations happened in fragments—texts sent in between other distractions, replies delayed by hours, messages carefully worded before hitting "send."

But real-world conversations were different.

• They required **presence.** I had to listen—not just wait for my turn to talk.

• They required **patience.** There was no option to "skip" to the next topic like scrolling through a feed.

• They required **vulnerability.** There was no filter, no chance to curate my responses. Just me, unedited.

It was uncomfortable at first. But the more I leaned into it, the more I realized how much I had been missing.

The Power of Undivided Attention

One day, I made a small but intentional change:

When I met up with someone, I left my phone in my bag.

At first, it felt unnatural. My hands twitched. I felt the urge to check it, to see if I was missing something. But then, something incredible happened:

I started truly **seeing** people again.

I noticed the way their eyes lit up when they talked about something they loved.

I noticed the subtle shifts in their expressions—the things they didn't say out loud.

I noticed the warmth that comes from being completely present with another human being.

For years, I had been dividing my attention—half in the real world, half in the digital one. And now, for the first time in a long time, I was **all in.**

And it made me wonder: **How much had I missed? How many moments had I let slip by because I wasn't really there?**

Repairing Relationships in the Real World

Stepping away from social media didn't just change how I connected with strangers online.

It changed how I connected with the people who mattered most.

- **With my family.** I started calling instead of texting. At first, it felt unnecessary—why call when I could send a message? But hearing their voices, the laughter, the little pauses between words—it reminded me how much richer real conversations are.

- **With my friends.** Instead of keeping up through posts and updates, I started **showing up.** Meeting for coffee. Sitting for hours, talking about things that didn't fit in a caption. And I realized: These weren't just "catch-ups." They were moments of true connection.

- **With strangers.** Without my phone as a barrier, I started making eye contact again. I smiled at people in passing. I had small, seemingly insignificant conversations with baristas, cashiers, people in line at the grocery store. And it hit me: *this* was the human experience—these tiny moments of connection that we ignore when we're buried in our screens.

I had spent years thinking that social media was what kept me connected.

But in reality, it had been keeping me at a distance.

Learning to Be Alone—Without Feeling Lonely

One of the biggest fears I had about unplugging was **loneliness.**

Without digital distractions, I thought I'd feel isolated. Disconnected. Forgotten.

But instead, something unexpected happened.

I realized that **solitude isn't the same as loneliness.**

When I was constantly online, I was never truly *alone*—but I wasn't fully present, either. I was always in this weird in-between state, half-engaged with the world but never really *there*.

Now, when I was alone, I was *truly* alone. And instead of feeling empty, I started to feel something else: **peace.**

I learned how to enjoy my own company again.

- I sat with my thoughts instead of drowning them in noise.
- I found hobbies that didn't involve a screen—reading, writing, even just sitting outside and watching the world go by.

- I let myself be bored without immediately reaching for my phone.

And in that stillness, I realized something I had forgotten:

Being alone is not something to fear. It's something to cherish.

The Depth of Real Connection

A few months into my detox, I had dinner with an old friend.

We sat for hours, talking, laughing, telling stories—not distracted, not half-present, but *fully* there.

At one point, they paused, smiled, and said:

"*You're different. You're really here.*"

And that was it.

That was the moment I knew this wasn't just a detox anymore.

This was **a new way of living.**

The Lesson: The Best Connections Happen Offline

Technology isn't evil. Social media isn't inherently bad. But they had convinced me that they were the *only* way to stay connected.

And that was a lie.

Real connection isn't measured in likes, comments, or message threads.

It's in the warmth of a hug. The sound of someone's laughter. The way a conversation unfolds when no one is in a rush to leave.

And the more I lived without the constant pull of my phone, the more I realized:

I don't want a life where my relationships are filtered through a screen.

I want a life where I'm **fully present.**

Where I don't just know about the people I love—I *experience* life with them.

Because at the end of the day, that's what really matters.

Not what we post. Not what we scroll through.

But the moments we actually *live*.

Part 3
The Awakening

Chapter 7
Rediscovering the Real World

At first, the real world felt foreign—too slow, too quiet, too unstructured. Without the constant flow of updates, messages, and notifications, I felt like I had stepped into a different timeline, one that moved at a pace I wasn't used to.

I had spent years inside the digital world, consuming information at breakneck speed. And now, suddenly, I was here. In real life. And I had no idea what to do with myself.

But then, something changed.

As I leaned into the stillness, I started noticing something I had overlooked for years:

The world outside my screen was still here.

And it was beautiful.

Relearning How to Live Without a Screen

I had spent so much of my life documenting experiences that I had forgotten how to just *experience* them.

Without my phone constantly in my hand, I started seeing life in a new way:

• **I walked without distractions.** Instead of staring at a screen, I looked at the sky. I noticed the way the wind moved through the trees, the way sunlight painted patterns on the sidewalk, the way strangers exchanged brief, passing smiles.

• **I ate without scrolling.** I had forgotten what it was like to taste food *fully*, without a screen competing for my attention.

• **I let myself be bored.** And instead of reaching for a distraction, I let my mind wander. That's when creativity came back—ideas, memories, reflections that I had buried under years of constant stimulation.

I had been so afraid of what I would lose by stepping away from technology. But now, I was realizing just how much I had **gained.**

The Joy of Doing Things for the Sake of Doing Them

One of the strangest, most unexpected shifts was how I started approaching hobbies again.

For years, everything I did had an unspoken pressure attached to it—if I read a book, I had to review it online. If I traveled, I had to post pictures. If I created something, I had to share it.

Everything had become performative.

But now, there was no audience. No pressure. No need to document or justify what I was doing.

And that changed everything.

- **I read books without summarizing them in a post.**
- **I took photos just for myself, not for likes.**
- **I wrote in a journal that no one else would ever see.**
- **I listened to music without sharing my playlist.**

For the first time in years, I was doing things simply because they *brought me joy*.

And I realized: **Not everything needs to be turned into content.** Some things are just meant to be lived.

Boredom: The Key to Creativity

At first, boredom felt like an enemy—an uncomfortable void that I instinctively wanted to fill.

But then, I remembered something:

Boredom is where creativity begins.

When I stopped filling every spare moment with scrolling, something unexpected happened:

- My mind started wandering again.
- I started thinking more deeply.

- I had ideas—real, original thoughts that weren't influenced by an algorithm.

For the first time in years, my creativity wasn't reactive. I wasn't just consuming and regurgitating content—I was **creating from within**.

I started journaling, sketching, writing, daydreaming.

Not because I had to. Not because anyone would see it.

But because it felt good.

And I realized: **I had been starving for this.**

Discovering the Power of Silence

Another thing I wasn't expecting?

How much my mind calmed down.

I hadn't realized how much anxiety the digital world had been feeding me.

- The endless noise.

- The constant comparisons.

- The pressure to respond, react, stay updated.

Without all of that, I felt lighter.

I started embracing silence.

I sat in coffee shops without my phone. I woke up and let myself *think* before reaching for a screen. I spent evenings in quiet reflection, rather than scrolling until my brain was numb.

And in that silence, I felt something I hadn't felt in years:

Peace.

Not the temporary, artificial peace that comes from zoning out on a screen.

But real, deep, lasting peace—the kind that comes from being fully present in your own life.

Seeing the World Through Fresh Eyes

One day, I went to a park I had been to a hundred times before.

But this time, I saw it differently.

I wasn't rushing through it, half-distracted by a podcast or text messages.

I was there. Fully there.

I watched the way the trees swayed in the wind.

I listened to the layers of sound—the birds, the laughter, the distant hum of traffic.

I felt the warmth of the sun on my skin, the texture of the grass beneath my hands.

And it hit me:

This world is so much more beautiful than anything on a screen.

For years, I had been *looking* at life through a phone. But now, I was actually *seeing* it.

And I never wanted to go back.

The Simple Beauty of Being Alive

I used to think that excitement only came from the digital world—the fast-paced, constantly changing, endlessly stimulating world of content, updates, and notifications.

But now, I saw excitement in the smallest things:

- The way a friend's face lights up when they talk about something they love.
- The feeling of deep, uninterrupted focus on a creative project.
- The way a quiet morning with a cup of coffee can feel like a sacred ritual.

I didn't need the internet to feel **alive** anymore.

I just needed to be **present.**

Choosing a Life That Feels Real

By stepping away from the digital world, I hadn't just broken an addiction.

I had **reclaimed my life.**

I had spent years living in a curated, hyper-connected, always-on world. And in doing so, I had forgotten what it felt like to live *fully*—to experience time, to embrace slowness, to be completely immersed in a moment.

But now, I knew the truth:

Real life is better than the internet.

It's richer.

It's deeper.

It's full of meaning in ways that can't be captured in a post.

And I had finally found my way back to it.

Chapter 8
The Challenges of Staying Unplugged

I thought once I unplugged, the hardest part would be over. That after breaking free from the grip of technology, life would simply fall into place—a peaceful, distraction-free existence where I would never again feel the pull of my phone.

I was wrong.

The real challenge wasn't quitting.

It was staying unplugged in a world that expects you to be connected.

The Pull of the Old Habits

At first, I was riding the high of my digital detox. I felt lighter, freer, more present than ever before. I swore I would never go back to my old ways.

But slowly, the pull began creeping back in.

- I'd pick up my phone just to check the time… and suddenly feel the urge to browse.

- I'd open my laptop to write, and before I knew it, my fingers were typing in the URL of a social media site—out of pure muscle memory.

- I'd feel a pang of curiosity—*What's happening in the world? What am I missing?*—and the temptation to check became overwhelming.

The addiction wasn't gone. It was just **waiting**.

And the worst part?

The world didn't help.

The Expectation to Be Online

We live in a world where **being unavailable is almost unacceptable.**

When I didn't respond to messages right away, people assumed I was ignoring them.

When I missed an event because I wasn't on social media, friends asked, "Didn't you see the invite?"

When I told people I wasn't on certain platforms anymore, they looked at me like I had admitted to living in a cave.

Everything—from friendships to work opportunities to news—flowed through the digital world.

And that made staying unplugged feel like swimming against the current.

No matter how much I wanted to stay away, **the world kept trying to pull me back in.**

The Fear of Being Left Out

For a while, I felt like an outsider.

Everyone else was still connected—sharing, posting, engaging in the online world while I stood on the sidelines.

At first, it was liberating. But then, the doubt crept in:

- *Am I isolating myself?*
- *Am I missing important conversations?*
- *Am I making my life harder by choosing to disconnect?*

I started questioning my decision.

Because the truth is, social media *does* serve a purpose. It *does* keep people in the loop. It *does* make networking easier, communication faster, information more accessible.

So I had to ask myself: **Was it really possible to stay unplugged... without becoming completely disconnected?**

Finding a Middle Ground

I didn't want to disappear from the world.

But I also didn't want to go back to being a slave to my phone.

So I had to figure out: **How do I exist in a digital world— without letting it control me?**

I started setting rules for myself:

- **No mindless scrolling.** If I opened my phone, I needed a reason. If I caught myself browsing out of habit, I put it down.

- **Limited time online.** I allowed myself to check social media *once a week*—not daily, not endlessly, just enough to stay informed without getting sucked in.

- **No phone during real-life interactions.** If I was with friends, my phone stayed in my bag. Period.

- **Offline alternatives.** Instead of messaging people on social media, I started calling. Instead of reading news online, I subscribed to physical magazines. Instead of watching random videos, I spent time creating.

I realized I didn't have to reject technology completely.

I just had to **control my relationship with it.**

Dealing with the Pressure to Return

Even with my new rules, the pressure didn't go away.

People still expected me to be available 24/7.

Friends still laughed when I said, "I didn't see that—I'm not on social media."

Companies still pushed me to engage, to brand myself, to *stay relevant*.

At times, I almost gave in.

Because the world doesn't make space for those who unplug.

But then I remembered why I started this journey in the first place.

I wasn't *missing out*.

I was gaining back my time, my focus, my peace of mind.

And no amount of digital convenience was worth trading that for.

The Reality of Staying Unplugged in a Hyper-Connected World

Here's the truth:

Quitting the digital world doesn't mean the world quits *you*.

- You will still feel the pull of old habits.
- You will still face pressure to stay online.
- You will still wonder if you're doing the right thing.

And some days, you might slip. You might check your phone out of boredom, fall back into old patterns.

But the difference now is **awareness.**

I no longer consume mindlessly. I no longer mistake online interactions for real connection. I no longer measure my life in likes and shares.

And that shift—**that freedom**—is worth every challenge.

Because at the end of the day, I don't want to be remembered for what I posted online.

I want to be remembered for the life I actually *lived*.

Part 4
A New Way of Living

Chapter 9
The Unexpected Lessons

When I first started this journey, I thought I was simply quitting social media. Taking a break. Unplugging for a while.

I had no idea how much it would change me.

I expected to feel less distracted. I expected to have more free time.

But what I didn't expect was how deeply this decision would reshape my mind, my relationships, and my understanding of what it truly means to live.

I didn't just disconnect from technology.

I reconnected with life.

And in that process, I learned lessons I never saw coming.

Lesson 1: Presence is a Superpower

For years, I had been living in fragments—half here, half somewhere else. Half in the conversation, half on my phone. Half experiencing a moment, half documenting it for others to see.

I thought I was multitasking. I thought I was staying connected.

But in reality, I was *never fully anywhere*.

Now, I see presence as a superpower.

- When I'm talking to someone, I listen—fully, without distraction.

- When I'm doing something, I immerse myself in it—without the urge to capture it for an audience.

- When I wake up, I experience the first moments of the day—before reaching for a screen.

And I've realized something profound: **life is richer when you are fully in it.**

The small details, the subtle emotions, the fleeting moments of beauty—those are the things I had been missing.

Not anymore.

Lesson 2: My Attention is My Most Valuable Resource

I used to think my time was my most valuable resource.

But I was wrong.

It's not just about how much time you have—it's about **what you do with your attention**.

Technology wasn't just stealing my time. It was fragmenting my focus, rewiring my brain to crave instant gratification, training me to jump from one thing to the next without truly absorbing anything.

Now, I guard my attention fiercely.

• I read books again—not just headlines or snippets, but full books, deeply and without distraction.

• I write without stopping to check notifications, allowing my thoughts to flow uninterrupted.

• I spend hours on creative projects, fully absorbed in the process.

And I've learned that deep focus—the kind where you lose yourself in something—is one of the most fulfilling states a person can experience.

But you have to protect it. Because if you don't, the world will take it from you.

Lesson 3: I Don't Need to Be Available 24/7

For years, I felt the pressure to always be **reachable**.

I had to respond to messages immediately. I had to check my email constantly. I had to be up to date on everything, all the time.

But stepping away made me realize:

Urgency is an illusion.

• Most messages don't need an instant reply.

• Most notifications don't matter.

• Most of the things I thought were "urgent" were just distractions in disguise.

Now, I **set boundaries**.

I check messages when *I* decide to.

I don't feel guilty for taking my time.

I no longer let the world dictate my pace.

And for the first time, I feel like I own my time—rather than letting it be owned by others.

Lesson 4: Real Connection is Built in Silence, Not in Notifications

Social media told me I was connected to hundreds, even thousands of people.

But the truth?

Real connection doesn't happen in likes, comments, or emojis.

It happens in **quiet moments.**

• Sitting with a friend in comfortable silence.

• Laughing over coffee without checking our phones.

- Hearing the sound of someone's voice instead of reading their texts.

Now, I prioritize **depth over quantity.**

I don't care how many people follow me. I care about the people who truly know me.

I don't care how many messages I get. I care about the conversations that actually mean something.

The world measures connection in numbers.

But I've learned that real connection can't be measured at all.

Lesson 5: I Am More Than My Online Identity

For years, I built a digital version of myself.

A profile. A persona. A curated collection of moments that represented *me*—or at least, the version of me I wanted people to see.

Stepping away from that world forced me to ask:

Who am I, when no one is watching?

- If I couldn't share my experiences, would they still matter?
- If I wasn't being validated by likes, would I still feel valuable?
- If I wasn't constantly "engaged," would I still exist?

The answer, I learned, is **yes.**

I don't need to document my life to make it meaningful.

I don't need external validation to know my worth.

I am not my social media presence. I am not my digital footprint.

I am **real.** And that is enough.

Lesson 6: Slow is Better Than Fast

The internet moves at an exhausting pace.

Everything is **now**—instant news, instant updates, instant responses. And for years, I tried to keep up.

But stepping away taught me the beauty of **slowing down.**

- Slower conversations are deeper.

- Slower meals taste better.

- Slower thoughts lead to more creativity.

- Slower days feel more meaningful.

I no longer feel the need to **rush** through life.

Because I've realized: the best moments—the ones that stay with you—aren't the ones you consume quickly.

They are the ones you savor.

Lesson 7: Happiness is in the Simple Things

I used to think happiness was about doing big, exciting things.

But now, I see it differently.

Happiness is in:

- A quiet morning with a cup of coffee.
- The way the sun feels on my skin.
- The smell of rain on pavement.
- The sound of a loved one's laughter.
- The deep satisfaction of finishing a good book.

For years, I chased excitement through screens, always looking for the next thing.

Now, I've learned that **joy isn't something you have to chase.**

It's right here. In the present.

You just have to slow down enough to notice it.

The Biggest Lesson of All

When I first unplugged, I thought I was losing something.

Now, I know the truth:

I wasn't losing anything. I was gaining everything.

- I gained clarity.
- I gained focus.
- I gained deeper relationships.
- I gained real, uninterrupted experiences.

* I gained a life that feels full—not because of what I post, but because of what I actually live.

The internet will always be there. The distractions will always exist. The temptation to return will never fully disappear.

But now, I know I have a choice.

And I choose **presence**.

I choose **depth**.

I choose **a life that feels real.**

Because at the end of the day, the best things in life?

They don't happen on a screen.

They happen **here.**

In the moments we choose to truly live.

Chapter 10
Rewired for Good

Breaking free from digital addiction wasn't just a temporary detox. It was a complete rewiring of my life, my habits, and my mindset.

I didn't just quit social media for a while.

I didn't just put my phone down for a few weeks.

I changed the way I interact with technology forever.

And in doing so, I found something I never expected: **freedom.**

Now, the challenge is **staying free.**

Because in a world that constantly tries to pull you back in— into the endless scroll, the notifications, the culture of distraction—**staying unplugged is an ongoing choice.**

A choice I have to make every single day.

. . .

The New Rules of Engagement

I didn't go completely off-grid. I didn't throw my phone into a lake and vow to live in the woods forever.

Instead, I built a **healthier relationship** with technology.

Here's how I stay unplugged—without disconnecting entirely:

1. I Use Technology as a Tool, Not a Trap

Technology isn't the enemy. The problem isn't that we use it—it's **how we use it.**

Now, I ask myself one simple question before I engage with any digital platform:

👉 **Am I using this tool, or is this tool using me?**

- I use my phone for essential tasks—not mindless scrolling.

- I use the internet to learn, not to escape.

- I use social media intentionally—only when I have a reason to be there.

If something is wasting my time, draining my energy, or pulling me away from real life? **I cut it out.**

2. I Control My Access to Screens

I used to feel like my phone controlled me.

Now, **I control it.**

- My phone **stays in another room** when I sleep. No late-night scrolling.

- I have **time limits** on certain apps. When my time is up, I'm done.

- I set **"no-screen zones"**—like meals, social gatherings, and early mornings.

By creating these boundaries, I stop my devices from dictating my life.

3. I Choose Depth Over Distraction

The biggest shift?

I no longer crave **quick hits of information.**

- I read long books instead of skimming articles.

- I have long, meaningful conversations instead of texting in fragments.

- I create more than I consume.

Distraction makes life feel **shallow**. But focus? Depth? Presence?

That's where real fulfillment is.

4. I Protect My Attention Like It's Gold

I no longer let my mind be hijacked by algorithms.

That means:

🚫 No notifications pulling me in.

🚫 No mindless browsing when I'm bored.

🚫 No wasting hours consuming content that doesn't add value.

My attention is **my most valuable resource**—and I guard it fiercely.

5. I Stay Unplugged—Even When the World Pulls Me Back

The hardest part of this journey?

The world doesn't want you to unplug.

People will expect instant replies.

Companies will push you to be online.

The digital world will keep inventing new ways to keep you hooked.

But now, I know I have **a choice.**

- **I don't have to participate in the distraction economy.**
- **I don't have to be constantly available.**
- **I don't have to live life through a screen.**

Instead, I choose to live **fully, intentionally, and in the real world.**

Encouraging Others to Unplug

This journey isn't just about me.

I've seen firsthand how powerful it is to reclaim your time, your attention, and your life. And I know there are so many people still trapped in the cycle—feeling lost, feeling drained, feeling like they can't break free.

So if you're reading this and wondering if you should unplug, too, let me say this:

- **You don't have to quit everything overnight.** Start small. Take a break. Delete one app. Set one boundary.

- **You don't have to disappear from the world.** You can stay connected—just in a way that serves *you*, not the algorithm.

- **You don't have to do what everyone else is doing.** The world may be addicted to screens, but *you* don't have to be.

Because here's the truth:

- The best moments of your life will never happen on a screen.

- The deepest conversations will never happen in a comment section.

- The most meaningful experiences won't come from a phone—they'll come from the real world.

So take the leap.

Unplug.

Reclaim your time.

Rewire your mind.

And start truly **living.**

Final Thought: The Life I Chose

I didn't just break free from digital addiction.

I chose a **new way of living**—one that is slower, deeper, and infinitely more meaningful.

Now, I don't wake up and check my phone first thing in the morning.

I don't feel the constant need to document my life.

I don't measure my worth in likes or followers.

Instead, I spend my days doing things that actually **matter** to me.

And for the first time in a long time, I feel **free.**

Not just from my phone.

Not just from social media.

But from the invisible chains that had been holding me back from truly experiencing life.

This journey wasn't about quitting technology.

It was about reclaiming **myself.**

And I wouldn't trade that for anything.

Your Invitation to Unplug

You don't have to quit everything overnight.

You don't have to delete all your accounts and live in the woods.

But you *can* take the first step.

- **Try going a day without social media.** Notice how it feels.
- **Turn off notifications.** Reclaim your attention.
- **Start setting boundaries.** Give yourself space to breathe.
- **Choose real conversations over digital ones.** See how deep they go.
- **Let yourself be bored.** You'll be surprised by what you discover.

And if you ever feel like you're missing out, just remember:

The best moments of your life will never happen on a screen.

They will happen in the world—the real one. The one waiting for you to come back to it.

So take a deep breath.

Put your phone down.

Step outside.

And start truly **living.**

Author's Note

When I first started this journey, I thought I was simply taking a break from social media.

I had no idea it would change everything.

I didn't just quit scrolling. I didn't just cut down on screen time.

I **rewired my entire relationship with technology**—and in doing so, I found something I never expected: **freedom.**

If you've made it to the end of this book, I hope you've seen that this isn't just my story.

It's **our** story.

We are all caught in the same web—pulled into an endless loop of notifications, engagement, and comparison. And yet, we *can* break free.

We *can* take back our time.

We *can* reclaim our focus.

Author's Note

We *can* choose a life that feels **real** instead of just looking good online.

It's not about rejecting technology altogether. It's about using it **with intention**—instead of letting it use us.

So if this book has inspired you, even in the smallest way, to unplug—to be more present, more mindful, more connected to the real world—then I've done what I set out to do.

Because this journey isn't just about escaping the digital addiction trap.

It's about choosing a life that feels **authentic, meaningful, and fully alive.**

And that?

That is worth everything.

Thank you for reading.

— Elliot Hayes

www.ingramcontent.com/pod-product-compliance
Lightning Source LLC
LaVergne TN
LVHW050025080526
838202LV00069B/6918